For The Grieving Child:
An Activities Manual

Written by Suzan E. Jaffe, Ph.D.

&

Illustrated by Jayme LaFleur

Printed in the United States of America

Library of Congress Data Block

Jaffe, Suzan
        For the Grieving Child: An Activities Manual by Suzan Jaffe

     ISBN   978-0-615-18355-8

          1.Grieving - children
          2.Coping with death
          3.Activities to help children cope with death.

Manufactured in the United States of America

Email: szjaffe@yahoo.com

Cover Design and interior illustrations: Jayme LaFleur

First Printing : 2004, Robbie Dean Press

Second Printing: 2008, Printed by Acme Bookbinding Co., Inc
                    Charlestown, MA

This book is dedicated to my son, Alex.

*His questions and sensitivity inspired me to write
this children's manual.*

In Memory of
*"Nanny," Ann Lee Jaffe, my mother-in-law, who will live on in the
pages of this book.*

Thanks and Appreciation
*To Gary, my dear husband, for his patience and understanding.
To: Fannie Fishlyn (my mom) for reading the text and providing
motherly support; my brother, Elliott Fishlyn, and sister, Debby
Carlton, for always telling me to believe in myself. Apprecia-
tion goes to my father-in-law, Dr. Norman Jaffe, whose prolific
skill helped edit the earliest draft. Special thanks to my friends
and colleagues: Bridget Weber, Karen Habib, Helene Fair, Ro-
berta Shapiro, Christine Damas, Steve Dudley, Paul Parisi, Judy
Silverstein, Debby Lucka, Arthur Spielman, Gerri Rudner, Rose-
mary Goldman, Richard Ferber, my tennis buddies, and my Fairy
Godmother, C. Leslie Charles--each one, in a very unique way,
contributed to this book's creation and delivery.*

NOTE TO ADULTS/PARENTS/GUARDIANS

PART I of this book is for children because they are the focus of this manual. To help facilitate the activities of this book, an adult should read PART II <u>first</u>. Even if the adult encourages an older sibling to sit and read with the younger one, still, the adult should have a clear understanding of this book's purpose and how it can be used effectively. PART II will give parents, caregivers, guardians, and professionals the information and tools to make the grieving experience more tolerable. So, please read PART II, NOW.

IMPORTANT NOTE

Make sure the environment is comfortable and conducive to quiet reading and performing the activities. For instance, shut off the TV or video movies/games. Soft background music is fine, but make sure it is not music that reminds your child of the deceased.

To make the activity sections of this book easier to complete, it is recommended that the reader gather all necessary supplies before sitting down with the child. Needed items are listed at the beginning of each chapter.

Table of Contents

Dedication

Note for ADULTS/PARENTS/GUARDIANS-- FIRST, Read Part II!

PART I

PART II

PART I

Introduction

Every life has a beginning and an ending. We call the beginning of life BIRTH and the ending of life DEATH. Be the living thing a beautiful daisy, a grasshopper, a dog, or a human being, the same rule holds true.

It is not supposed to be easy for you *or* for grown-ups when a family member or a friend dies, regardless of age or cause of death. No matter what the case may be, even though we know that no one can live forever, death is always hard to understand.

If you are reading this book, you have probably just found out that someone who was a part of your life has died. When someone special to you has died, a change in the way things "used to be" begins for you and for those around you. This time is called the *"grieving process."* There is no exact moment that this process (or way of feeling) begins, nor is there a specific time that it ends. Some people will have moments of grieving (feeling bad, angry, or sad) for the rest of their lives. But, grieving is not a really bad thing, nor is it something to be afraid of.

You may have questions or unfamiliar thoughts or feelings. Some of these thoughts and feelings may be uncomfortable.

This book was written to help you and your close family members after someone has

died. It might be a tough time for you and for the grown-ups that take care of you. It is a time for feeling sad, lonely, and confused - a time when you may really miss the person.

Each chapter of the activity book will begin with an insert describing what things you will need for the described activities. Gather these items before sitting down to read with your child. A pencil or erasable pen is recommended for any part of the book that requires writing or drawing. This way, the child can come back to certain parts and change or revise his/her original words or drawings.

CHAPTER 1: What Happens When A Person Dies?

Depending on your family's religious or spiritual beliefs, there will be different explanations for what actually happens to the person after he or she dies.

This is a very personal thing, and every family will have its own, private way of explaining this to you.

Some people believe that there is life after death. Not life, like we know life to be now, but somehow, someway, the person lives on...in an "after-life."

Others believe that the "soul" or spirit of the person lives on in another form after death...

...perhaps living on in the hearts or minds of the people who are continuing to remember him or her. You could think of it as the person *staying alive* in your memories.

3

Still others believe that after a person dies, they are reborn as another person,...**or reborn as an animal!**

CHAPTER 2: Different Ways to Grieve

There is no right way to grieve. There is no right way or best way to let go of the sadness or other feelings you have right now. There is no way to fast forward through this time. You can't press the rewind button either. We all need time to grieve.

Just like there is no right way to live through this time, there is no wrong way to grieve either. So, don't worry about making mistakes. There is no perfect length of time to grieve either. Grieving needs to be done in your own way and on your own time schedule.

Give yourself time...

Time to remember the good and the bad things about the person you have lost.

You need time to remember the fun times and the hard times that were part of your relationship with this person. Take time to talk about these feelings with your family and close friends.

Sometimes a person dies before you have a chance to say goodbye.

5

This happens when people die unexpectedly (in other words, when there is no warning - like with accidents). When you don't have a chance to say goodbye, it can make you feel like things are "unfinished," an empty feeling.

Missing the person, whether you expected him or her to die or not, can be hard at first, and may make you feel sad or have other painful feelings.

Depending on the religion and beliefs of your family, there will be certain rules about visiting the cemetery and grave of the person who died. There may not be a grave if your loved one was not buried, but cremated.

Cremation is what some people request to have done to their bodies once they have died. Their bodies are burned and only their ashes remain. These ashes are sometimes kept in the family's home in a special jar or vase called an urn.

Other times, the ashes are spread over a special place that the dead person had requested, such as a beautiful field, the ocean, a mountain top, or even buried in the corner of their family's yard.

When and if you feel like it, you might ask an adult what happened to the body, after he or she died. Don't be afraid to ask. Knowing rather than guessing about what happened might make grieving easier.

Reader may stop now and ask the following:

1. Do you want to talk about any of what we've just read?

2. Am I frightening you with any of this information?

3. Do you have any worries that we haven't talked about yet?

4. If you don't feel like talking, you can write things down here or on a separate piece of paper. If you want, we can talk about your feelings later.

_____

_____

_____

_____

_____

_____

_____

_____

_____

_____

_____

_____

_____

CHAPTER 3 - What Are All These Feelings?

Sometimes, you may feel angry, other times mad, or you may feel this achy feeling inside. Don't be afraid of all these unusual feelings. Don't ignore how you feel. If you can let out these inside feelings, do so. This is a natural part of grieving - so however you feel - it is ALL OK!

It's even OK to laugh!

Sometimes when grown-ups are dealing with the death of a close friend or family member, they may act differently and sort of "not normal". Like you, they are having their own difficulties getting used to missing the person who died. They ache too, and may feel lonely or confused, just like you.

You don't need to forget the person to feel better. You don't need to stop loving him or her either. Remembering the good times you shared with the person is helpful during this time called "grieving". People often talk only about the nice things and times they shared with the person that died, but what about the arguments? What

about the arguments? What about the times you were unhappy or disappointed with the person? What about the times this person punished you? It's perfectly all right to talk about the bad times. In fact,

talking about these times may lessen some of the uncomfortable, achy, or sad feelings you have and actually help you through the grieving process.

Sometimes, you might feel better if you give or receive a hug. Don't be afraid to ask for one.

Hugs are great medicine!

Hugs can be one of the most
healing gifts of life.

ACTIVITY #1
Drawing Faces

Items needed for activity: crayons, colored markers,
drawing paper, pencils, erasers
(when drawing in faces, use erasable pencils or pens)

Sometimes drawing can make you feel better. Each type
of face shows two examples. The empty face is for you to
fill in.

CAN YOU DRAW A HAPPY FACE?

 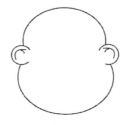 

CAN YOU DRAW A SAD FACE?

 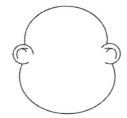 

NOW, DRAW A MAD FACE

 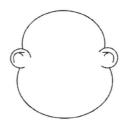 

WHAT OTHER FACES WOULD YOU LIKE TO DRAW?

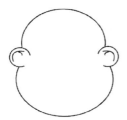  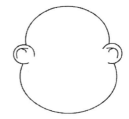

Can you draw your face?

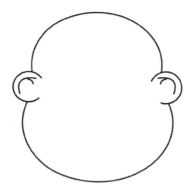

Sometimes there is a weird or empty feeling inside. It is very common for people to cry after someone dies. It may even feel like your heart is crying...

...or it may feel like you have a stomachache.

Some children do not feel anything at all, and that's fine too.

Remember:

There is no right or wrong way to feel.

Sometimes, grown-ups don't want to show us that they feel scared, angry, sad, or lonely after someone close to them has died. Typically, they don't want you to see them cry. They might think that if you know how they truly feel, that you will get more scared. So, they try to put on a "happy face"...but you can tell that it's not their real face!

The truth is that grown-ups have the same feelings as children have, but have learned to behave in a certain way over the years. Some grown-ups have learned good ways of dealing with bad news, like death, others have not...many are still learning.

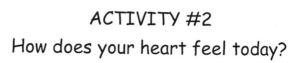

ACTIVITY #2
How does your heart feel today?

Please color the heart below any way you like.

CHAPTER 4: Exercise & Sports

Sometimes, during the grieving process, it feels good to get out and exercise or play your favorite sport.

What kinds of sports do you enjoy?

Do you like to run?

Swing?

Play Soccer?

Jump?

Play ping-pong?

Play catch?

Play tennis?   Bounce?

What about swimming or fishing?

Basketball?

Water play?

Make a list of all the sports and games you enjoy on the lines below:

_____

_____

_____

_____

_____

How soon do you think you'd like to play this sport or game again? Or
how soon would you enjoy learning a new game or sport?

_____

_____

_____

_____

_____

Having plans to learn new things or return to playing the sports you used
to enjoy can help you feel better. Looking forward to having fun again
can make a big difference in how you feel today.

CHAPTER 5: Music

Some children don't care much for outdoor sports, but enjoy listening to music. Some children like to write their own music. Others play musical instruments.

Do you play an instrument?

If you do play an instrument, practicing may help while you are grieving. If you don't feel like practicing, it is understandable, but surprisingly playing your instrument might make you feel better. Give it a try!

Try playing just 2 minutes today and add a minute or two each day till you reach 15 or 20 minutes daily.

If you don't play an instrument, you can listen to music. Turn on the radio, a musical video, or a CD. Try dancing a little; just let loose; go crazy! If no one minds, turn up the music as loud as you like. Ask an adult to join you, it might help him or her feel better too.

CHAPTER 6: Day-By-Day Feelings

Check the boxes that describe how you feel right now:
(use pencil to fill in, so you can erase and fill in another time again)

☐ Sad

☐ Guilty

☐ Unfair

☐ Angry

☐ Don't feel like talking to anyone

☐ Confused, confusion

☐ Numb feeling

☐ Poor appetite

☐ Miserable

☐ Blame

☐ Feel like something is wrong

☐ Feel like crying a lot

☐ Lonely, loneliness

☐ Trouble concentrating

☐ Can't believe this has happened

☐ Trouble sleeping

Sadness

If you feel sad, crying is one way to get the sad feelings out. It's a good thing to do. Even grown-ups cry when someone dies.

Try it!

21

Guilt

Do you feel guilty? Do you ever think it is your fault that the person you are grieving for has died? It is never anyone's fault. When you break something, you may feel responsible; you may actually be to blame, especially if you were playing with something that you'd been told not to touch. But accidents happen and when they do, we feel bad. That is what guilt feels like...

...and looks like.

Control

When someone dies and you are grieving, there is often a feeling of losing control. You did not have any say in his or her death and you cannot prevent these kinds of tragedies. Death is not something we have much control over. So, it is important to think about what you CAN control in your life, rather than thinking about how many things you CAN'T control. It will make you feel stronger and less afraid knowing that there are many things you CAN control.

Can you think of some things that you do control? For instance:

I can watch my favorite TV shows
every Saturday morning.

I like to eat cereal for breakfast
on Tuesdays.

Can you think of 5 more things that you have control over?

(use pencil here so you can erase and fill in again on a different day)

1. _____

2. _____

3. _____

4. _____

5. _____

By feeling more in control, you might feel better in a situation that

seems out of control.

23

When A Friend Dies

What if a close friend of yours has died? This really stinks. How can you feel good about playing with your other friends when your good friend is dead? How can you be happy and play with the toys you used to play with him or her?

Probably not today, but in time you'll find that even though it is hard, it is OK to play, laugh, and have fun with your other friends, or even make some new friends.

You may say to yourself, I feel guilty playing with (name of someone new). There may be a feeling of guilt or shame that you are trying to replace your friend with someone new. But, this doesn't have to be. Your friend can live on in your thoughts, in your heart, and in the many memories that you had with him or her.

Finding a new friend and enjoying your new friend is a good thing and very OK. It is an important step towards feeling better.

CHAPTER 7: Uncomfortable Feelings

Activity #3
Silly Putty® Fun

Items needed for activity - Silly Putty® - can be any brand

Take the Silly Putty® in your hand and squish it, throw it, bounce it, make it into a long worm, or make several little worms...

...Squeeze it, pull it apart, see how thin it will get before it breaks apart. Do anything you want with it; it'll feel good. You can take some comics and copy them onto the putty, too. See how many things you can do with it!

Activity #4
Clay Therapy

Items needed for activity - Use any type of clay for this
activity - Play-Doh® products or similar are also fine

Take a big blob of clay. You
can use the colors separately
or mix...them together.

- build up a mound and squash
  it, or mold it into something...

- ask a grown up to help you with this next part:
  * Take a plastic bag and open it up (use scissors to cut the sides
    so that it covers a large enough area to prevent damage to the
    flooring)
  * Put the opened plastic bag on the floor
  * Stand and take globs of clay and throw the clay as hard as you
    can onto the plastic
  * Scream out or yell - say whatever you want - let out any feel-
    ings you may have inside, as you throw the globs of clay
  * Invite a parent, relative, or friend (no matter how old) to
    join in this activity
  * This activity is a very good way to express your feelings in a
    healthy way, a way that does not hurt anyone

Activity #5

The Meaning of Colors

(Note: please use pencil to complete this activity so you can erase and fill in on another day)

Different colors can make you feel a variety of ways. Colors may hold different meanings for your friends, and your own feelings may change depending on your mood. For example, the color blue can mean cool or sad. The color red may mean mad or hot. Brown can give you a lazy or low feeling. Green can remind you of grass or trees. Pink often brings a cheery feeling.

What do these and other colors mean to you?

GRAY_____

RED_____

PINK_____

BLUE_____

ORANGE_____

BROWN_____

PURPLE_____

GREEN_____

On the next few pages, take some crayons or markers and draw some colorful pictures.

Be creative and have fun!

Draw whatever you like.

CHAPTER 8 - Missing Hurts

When someone you know has died it is normal to miss him or her. How much you miss someone is your private business and no one else's. When you miss someone, it is OK to say so, to speak up and say what's on your mind.

Talking is good for you!

Talking is an important step in the grieving process - so TALK, TALK, TALK...

Maybe you could go for a walk and talk.

You may choose to talk with a parent, another relative, your pet dog, cat, fish, or even to one of your stuffed animals.

Talking about your feelings with other children your own age can help, too. Sharing your thoughts and worries can make them seem less troubling and less frightening.

CHAPTER 9 - "Take a Moment or Two"

Sometimes it helps just to stop what you are doing and take a "moment". Taking a "moment" means doing anything to stop, to *pause*, and to take a break from your routine day.

Maybe, you just need to STOP now and then and just take a fresh look at things.

After someone dies, it is natural to miss this person a lot and have a *hurt-ing* feeling inside. Taking a "moment" or two may help ease the pain from this kind of hurting or missing.

Here is a list of some things you can do that should help with these feelings. Not all of these ideas will be right for everyone - so pick the ones that are right for you or make up your own.

Activity #6
Ways to take "moments"

Tell a story about the person who died

Sit on a bench and just sit, talk, sing, whistle, or even hum

Walk along a stream

Feed birds or squirrels

Go to the beach

Hike a mountain

Visit a beautiful garden

Swing on a swing

These "moments" can help you with times that you need to share what's on your mind. Taking a "moment" to sit and think about the person that died can help you through the grieving process. You can do this with a friend, a parent, or other relative, or if you prefer, you can take moments alone.

Remember:

If you feel sad - say so - CRY

If you feel mad - say so - SCREAM

If you feel angry - say so - PUNCH A PILLOW

If you feel scared - say so - ASK FOR HUGS

If you feel upset - say so - TALK ABOUT IT

If you feel sorry for yourself - say so - It's OK to feel sorry for yourself, but find someone to sit with and talk about your feelings

Maybe it's time to take a "moment".

When you are grieving, in addition to talking and taking "moments", there are many other things you can do. The activities on the following pages have some good examples.

Activity #7

More things to do when grieving

1) Draw a picture
for the person who died

2) Write a letter to the person
who died

Even though he or she will not be able to read your letter or see your picture, it may help YOU just by DOING it - it can help just by getting your private feelings on paper. If you don't know how to write yet, ask a grown-up, friend, or other family member to write the words on the paper for you.

If the person you are grieving is buried, if permitted, ask a grown-up to take you to the cemetery. Leave some flowers.

Write a letter and leave
it at the grave...

...or a photograph...

...a favorite toy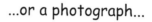
or a stuffed animal.

3) Take a walk with a grown-up, and along the way take turns remembering different things about the person. You may want to remember things that made you laugh, and then talk about something that bothered you or made you mad...when the person was still alive.

4) Plant something and watch

life begin

> For this activity you will need one of the following: flowering seeds, a small cutting from a flowering plant or bush, an avocado seed, a sunflower seed or an apple seed; planting soil, a small pot

Have a grown-up help you plant a seed or a plant so that you may watch it grow. Make sure to water it when needed and put it in enough sunlight, so that it will grow. It may take many weeks, but be patient and tend to this new life daily.

Watching your seed blossom into a plant or flower may make you feel better. Enjoy this chance to grow a living thing. The flower cannot replace your lost one, but it may make you feel a little better. You have begun a new life by planting your seed, and now, by taking good care of your plant, you can enjoy watching it grow.

CHAPTER 10 - Moments & Memories

After someone close to you dies, your life may seem to have stopped...it may feel very hard to move ahead and return to your regular life and daily routines. No matter how bad you might feel today, most people feel better as time goes on. Time helps most people, young and old.

Some people take many days or weeks to feel better, for others it takes many months. It may even take a year to feel "normal" again.

Your memories of the person who is now gone from your world can and will live on...just in another form. Take time to think of him or her; take a "moment" or two to remember with a close friend or family member.

Even though things may seem pretty strange or different now, you will not always feel just like you do right now. You will have many years of happiness in the future. Even though this time of griev-

ing is difficult, you will get through it. Hopefully, it will not be too long before you are feeling better and can get back to the things you loved doing before.

PART II

1.   Introduction - Why This Book?

This two-part book was written to fill a void that I discovered after my mother-in-law died. My son, Alex, then seven years-old, had many questions about her death, but particularly about how he was supposed to behave during the time that we "grown-ups" call the "grieving" or "mourning" period, the time following death and other significant losses. As a concerned mother and health care professional, I decided to hit the bookstores and the library in search of an appropriate, child-friendly book, but was disheartened by what I found.

Some books I found were written to explain the meaning of death, others to help children prepare for the pending loss. Some discussed deaths of an expected nature, such as following a prolonged illness. Some focused on deaths of a sudden nature, due to accidents, murder, or suicide. Other children's books were fictional stories that told stories about dying, death, and loss, but used fictional human characters or animals to convey under-lying points.

To my surprise and disappointment, there was little that offered help and guidance to the parents and at the same time provided simple explana-tions to a young child. This book was written to fill that void and to empower young children. I believe that this book will assist children and at the same time provide you, the parent (or guardian), with a valuable resource.

Understand, that this book has not been written to make the grief go away - nor to deny the sadness (or multitude of other feelings) that accompany grief. Hopefully, this book will help you become aware of your child's worries and concerns and in turn help your child through this often dif-ficult and painful process. I hope this book makes it easier for children to ask questions and to express feelings that may be confusing, unfamiliar, or uncomfortable.

Older children (over 10 years old) may choose to read Part I alone and only ask you for help if they have questions. A teenager may find it meaningful to sit with a younger sibling, relative, or friend and read the book and do the hands-on activities together. This way, they can relate on a child-to-child level, rather than grown-up to child.

Be sensitive to your child's frame of mind and emotional comfort level. Try not to rush through any particular section. Allow your child time to ask questions, perform the activities, and take breaks.

2.   What is the grieving process?

The "grieving process" is a term used to describe the time following a significant loss. People can grieve loss due to death of a human or of a pet. People also grieve other losses, such as occurs following a divorce, a move, a loss of job etc... This book is primarily concerned with human loss, that which is experienced after a person dies.

Following a death, people of all ages go through various stages of mourning and adapting to life without the person who has died. Regardless of age, children and adults can never be fully prepared to lose someone who was integrally involved in their lives, be it a parent, sibling, grandparent, or friend. In today's society it is not that uncommon for a grandparent to be one of the primary caretakers, if not the primary caretaker of a young child. Losing a grandparent in these circumstances may have a similar impact as that of losing a parent. Similarly, if the child is raised with a live-in nanny, housekeeper, or Au pair, and this person dies, the grief may be of a devastating nature.

For every child there is a unique set of individuals who holds special meaning and place in their hearts. It is impossible to predict how each of us will grieve when the time comes. It's not one of those things in life that if you practice it, it gets easy. Grieving is not something that has a finite ending. Grieving the loss of someone close to us changes in form as our life goes on, but may never end for some.

3.   What is anticipatory grief?

This type of grief usually occurs during a prolonged terminal illness. It does not eliminate the post death grieving process, but sometimes may give it a "jump-start." Some people feel that nothing of this sort can really occur. Others believe that watching someone during the terminal stages of illness can somehow better prepare them for death. It simply means that a person begins a process of detachment before the individual dies. In other words, they are getting used to being "without" the individual.

If a young child has observed an older family friend or a grandparent sick and deteriorating over a long period of time, the child might feel relieved at the time of the person's death. Having watched the person change in appearance and behavior is often a depressing and scary experience for a child - let alone an adult.

If the seriously ill individual is no longer able to communicate with the family, other family members (out of necessity) take over any roles and/or responsibilities of that individual. In this capacity, the family has filled the dying person's place, despite still being among the "living". So even though he or she is living, he or she is no longer a participating member of the family. One can think of this anticipatory grief as "this is what it will be like when s/he is dead".

Those who believe that anticipatory grief does occur still have the task of continuing to support and love the person during this terminal phase of life, i.e. not to detach completely. Others feel that it would be impossible to give "love or support" if grieving occurs on any level while the person is still living. This is a very personal issue, and there are no rules or rights and wrongs here.

4.   Why is it so hard to talk about the person that has died?

Rarely does anyone want to face the reality of death or talk about it. Children need straightforward answers when discussing death. For most people, young and old, it is an uncomfortable and somewhat foreign subject. Simple honesty is still the best option.

The discomfort associated with discussing death is attributed to our general fear of it. Talking about death and how we feel when a person dies is trying because most of us have little personal experience with it. Most young children have not had to experience death, so the first one is often the hardest. Being open about death and talking about it with your child provides a better understanding of what it is and can decrease associated fears.

5.   How do I teach or help my child grieve?

Children will grieve at their own rates. You cannot rush into having them express how they feel. In fact, during the immediate time after the death, the shock and denial of death may cause children simply to be unable to grasp the concept at all. The notion that they will never see that person again is beyond their capability.

To be supportive to your child during this time, it is important that you have some understanding of your own feelings concerning the loss. First of all, there is no best way or right way to grieve, and there is no wrong way either. Mourning the loss of a person who was important to you and to your young child needs to be done in your own way and on your own time schedule.

Try not to ask a lot of questions of the youngster. Too many questions and too much information too soon can backfire. The child needs to be given time and space to work through his or her unique feelings, and you need to give yourself time as well. You and your child should spend time remembering the good and the bad about the person - the positive and the negative - about your relationship. You need time to talk about these feelings with your close friends and family.

For adults and children, one of the most important challenges after someone dies is to work through the pain or anger that accompanies grief. This is because no one enjoys feeling "bad" - especially children. When we speak of experiencing "pain," we are not talking about physical pain, but emotional pain. This is a very difficult concept to explain to children as they may have an "unpleasant" feeling, but don't understand what has just happened. This is one of the reasons that it is so much easier to avoid discussing any of this.

There is no way to fast forward the grieving process, though the length of this period may vary greatly. For many, one year seems to bring completion, for others much more time is required. Periodic moments of grief may be felt for the rest of the person's life.

Children need to have an opportunity to share their feelings and voice their fears. This will help them cope and understand the grieving process.

6. Common feelings children have when someone dies

GUILT

Guilt is a common feeling that children experience after someone dies. They may ask: "Did Uncle Harry die because of something I did? He was really mad at me yesterday for breaking his eyeglasses. Did that make him die?" The child may imagine that had s/he behaved differently the person would still be alive. Sometimes, children see sadness in their parents when they, themselves, don't feel sad. This may cause a child to feel guilty - guilty that they feel nothing. The guilt may intensify if they observe their loved ones crying, irritated, easily upset, or distressed.

FEAR

Some children may fear being left alone in their rooms, or even with a baby sitter during this time. Other fears may surface as well, including bad dreams or restless sleep. If a child loses a parent or a sibling, it is usually a shocking and traumatic experience. How much to tell a child about the death of a parent or sibling is clearly one of the most difficult and sensitive conversations an adult can ever have. When both parents are deceased or if one of the parents is estranged from the child, it will be essential to find someone else with whom the child can vent, for instance, a close relative, grandparent, older cousin, minister. It is best that whoever tells the child about the death has had a trusting relationship with the child.

If one parent or grandparent dies, the child may fear that the other parent may also die. This makes it very difficult for the surviving parent to leave the child with someone else. A young child may fear that s/he will be or-phaned. If a sibling or parent were killed in an automobile accident, the grieving child may become terrified of going in cars.

When the fear is less defined and the child just feels generally anxious, he may ask if he can stay home from the school or, if not yet of school age, s/he may ask you to stay home from work. The child may develop difficulty fall-ing asleep or may develop recurring nightmares. S/he may ask you to stay in his or her bedroom, not go out in the evening or, if school age, s/he may fake illness, in order to stay home from school.

A child may voice new worries to you or an older sibling. It is very important, and it is recommended that the child expresses these and all fears. It is not uncommon, however, that when a parent dies, the child may wish that someone he didn't like had died instead.

HIDING FEELINGS

It is not uncommon for adults to hide their feelings. Even if the audience is his or her family, they may take the stance: I must appear "strong" for those present. This way of dealing with grief is not necessarily the best choice for adults and is not advised for children. Children must be free to express how they feel, and they should be encouraged to do so. Keeping one's feelings bottled up inside may backfire. Expressing how you feel, as long as you don't go overboard, will give the child an open door, permission in other words, to express their fears and worries to you.

Many "psychosomatic" (emotionally caused) illnesses may be caused by turning feelings inward, keeping the stress within, instead of vocalizing and letting them out. Keeping feelings inside can also make them become even bigger than they are and may make a person feel even more apprehensive. Don't be embarrassed to say how you feel, don't be ashamed of how you feel - just be yourself.

A child's behavior may appear resilient after the death, i.e. he seems "normal" within a short period of time. You may observe a "business as usual" behavior. Do not be fooled since such behavior may be the child's way of trying to deny the reality of the loss. Suppression of grieving pain may develop into a more difficult period down the road. Word of another's death, even a person who was unknown to the child (such as what might be seen on TV news), can stir up unresolved issues for the child and initiate a new period of grief. Even if the child seems fine, the activities in this manual are an opportunity for your child to express hidden feelings in a caring, supportive, secure, and loving environment.

Children learn from their adult role models. Grieving is no different. Children must learn from us that when a person dies we cannot replace them, like we might replace a broken toy. What we can do, however, is teach our children to remember the things about the person that made him or her so special. Perhaps, there was an activity that they particularly enjoyed doing with this person. Enjoy that activity with your child and remember him or her during the activity. Let your child know that it's OK to have fun or laugh while you are playing the game or doing the activity.

CONFUSION

Children can feel very confused at these times. For example, if the child played tennis with his dad and now his dad has died, the confused child may ask, "How can I play tennis without daddy? How can I enjoy tennis?" Certainly, it is expected that the child would and should think of his father. This will be very difficult at first. It is expected and quite normal for the child to resist playing this sport for some time after the death. But, in time s/he should be encouraged to do so again, with another close family member, coach, or friend. S/he can be reminded that dad loved this sport, that dad loved to play with him and that he *would want* his son to continue. In time, the child will learn that it is OK to play tennis and enjoy the sport that he used to play with his dad. Victories will be met with celebration instead of sadness.

Sometimes, when grown ups are dealing with death, they act differently, and this causes confusion for their children. We adults experience our own hard task of grieving. Emotional maturity will allow an adult to appreciate these changes (in his or her own behavior), but a child may witness the adults around him in a curious and confused way. They may wonder, "Why is mommy or daddy acting so weird?" Any variance from the adult's usual behavior will confuse the child. As an adult, if you know you are behaving in an atypical manner, be prepared for your children to take note and have your explanations ready.

SAFETY ISSUES

Most importantly, your child needs to feel safe. S/he needs your love, your strength, and your warmth. Above all, s/he needs to know that no matter how bad s/he feels, you will be there and you will not leave him/her. S/he needs to know that s/he shouldn't be afraid to tell you how s/he feels and that everything will be OK. As an adult, you might think: wait, how can I say this? I have fears, too; maybe I will have an accident and die?

We cannot and should never share our anxieties about our own mortality with a young child. A young child cannot handle this burden. So even if you (for whatever reason) do not feel safe, *say you do*. Act confident; act like you are omnipotent and powerful.

You can and should show emotion regarding the recent loss. The grieving process can be a healing experience for you as well as your child. Do not add to the burden of introducing... "Aunt Sophie is so sick; I'm worried she may die too... or gee, with all the terrorism today I fear sending you to school." Statements like these will only generate fear and increase your child's sense of insecurity.

7.   Does grieving ever end?

Grieving is a process that takes several steps to complete - it is not a single event or episode. Unfortunately, there is no recipe for this process, and there is no set rule that states that everyone must experience every stage in the same order. Some professionals feel that the work of grieving is complete when the deceased is not constantly thought about as an absence in the mourner's daily thoughts, but has come to rest firmly within one's heart or mind (memories). The memory of the person can then live on in one's consciousness forever. Others will tell you that they feel "ready" to participate in their favorite hobbies or sports again. Still others, particularly those who have lost a spouse, will resume dating.

For a young child, grieving may go through many phases. Just when you think your child is ready to move on, to resume his or her regular daily activities, the child may have a sudden relapse. For instance, after returning to school, things may have been going along smoothly. Then, you receive a call from the teacher that your child has been disruptive, combative, or crying during class. This would signify that more time is needed and that the grieving process is ongoing. This is not a reason to remove the child from school, but perhaps reason to seek professional intervention.

8.   Anxiety and Depression

You might find that when reading this manual with your child, s/he seems very interested at first and then simply walks away or displays anger.

This may be a sign of increased anxiety. Young children do not have the ability to identify "oh...I must be feeling stressed now" - they just feel uncomfortable, troubled, and frustrated.

Feeling anxious is not a good feeling...at any age. Young children do not have the cognitive maturity to understand these feelings, and it is easy for the anxiety to have secondary effects. Some signs of increasing anxiety include: temper tantrums, inattention, fighting, poor listening, school problems, or sleeping difficulties. Other signs of underlying anxiety or depression are demonstrated by a lack of interest in activities that the child used to enjoy, such as playing musical instruments, sports, or even video games.

Sometimes, children will not say much about the death after it occurs and will actually seem quite "normal". Yet, weeks or months later, they will appear angry, sad, or depressed. This may be subtle, in that a child may not tell you directly how he or she feels, but you may note a change in behavior, sleeping, or eating habits. A child might even feel so angry or upset that trouble at school or fights with friends occur.

For an adult, the deepest sense of loss may occur on the anniversary of the person's death or birthday. A very young child may not be aware of these milestones, but if the death occurred on their birthday or an important holiday (e.g. Christmas, Chanukah, or Thanksgiving), he or she may experience a renewal of sad feelings on that day. If so, it may be very difficult for children to celebrate this holiday.

Be aware of warning signs that may alert you to the onset of clinical depression, which can occur even in very young children. Some of the most common signs and symptoms include: extreme sadness, crying for prolonged periods, and an acute change in sleeping, eating, or toileting habits.

If your child becomes melancholy, withdrawn, cries for long periods of time, sleeps very little, sleeps in increasing amounts, or expresses suicidal thoughts, you should consult a professional. After consulting your pediatrician, a referral to a psychologist or psychiatrist may be recommended. Do not ignore behaviors that may lead to a lethal situation.

Warning signs of depression

- Total denial of the death - still looking for the person
- Panic attacks (during daytime or during sleep)
- Severe unrelenting sadness
- Persistent difficulty sleeping
- Relentless misbehaving
- Grades suffering
- Withdrawal from friends and family
- Refusal to play favorite sport or other games
- Drug or alcohol use (seen in teens)
- Suicidal thoughts or actions (reason for immediate professional intervention)

9.   Comforting the Comforter

Children need to be comforted, but at the same time, parents need to be comforted and can be comforted by their children. Grieving children often feel scared and as the adult our job is to help alleviate these fears.

After my mother-in-law died, my son and I would take time to sit and reflect. During these times we would say things either about her (we called her Nanny) or we chose to think quietly to ourselves. The act of "taking a moment" should never become a forced activity. You can always choose to skip your turn, i.e. "I don't need to take a moment now or I don't want to take a moment now, maybe later." A "moment" might take another form - for instance, in my case, my son felt that thinking about his tennis game or telling a funny joke was also OK. Other times he would say, "Thinking about Nanny makes me sad. Do I have to take a moment now?" Of course not. No activity should be forced on a young child, and not every activity will be appropriate for every child.

10.   Conclusion

We must educate and console our children, and we need to initiate conversations between them and ourselves. Eventually, the grieving process will help even the youngest child move-on. By taking moments and rekindling our memories of the deceased, our children will endure the grieving process together with us.

In closing, I'd like to share the following personal experience. This event is one that contributed wholeheartedly to my commitment to write this book.

My son, Alex, referred to his grandmother as Nanny. Nanny died on the 5th night of the Jewish Festival of Lights, Chanukah, when customarily the 5th candle is lit. The candles are lit in a special candle holder, called a Menorah. According to Jewish tradition, because she died on this day of Chanukah, this candle will never burn out; it will shine for her forever. Knowing this religious belief was very comforting for Alex when he was seven years-old. On succeeding Chanukahs, we have always said a special prayer for Nanny on the 5th night of this holiday, and we light a special candle (called a Yartzite candle) in her honor. We all take a "moment" and remember her, and for that moment she is with us again.

Supplemental Reading List

Dougy Center, The. (1999). *35 ways to help a grieving child.* Portland, OR: The National Center for Grieving Children & Families.

Fitzgerald, H. (1992). *The grieving child--a parent's guide.* New York: Simon and Shuster.

Fry, V. L. (1995). *Part of me died, too.* New York: Dutton Children's Books, Division of Penguin Books.

Gellman, M. Rabbi, & Monsignor Hartman, T. (1999). *A kid's book for living through loss.* New York: Morrow Junior Books.

Heegaard, M. (1988). *When someone very special dies--children can learn to cope with grief.* Minneapolis, MN: Woodland Press.

James, J. W., R. Friedman, with Dr. L. M. Quill. (2001). *Why children grieve--for adults to help children deal with death, divorce, pet loss, moving and other losses.* New York: Imprint of Harper Collins Pub.

Johnson, J., & Dr. M. Johnson. (1998). *Children grieve, too--helping children cope with grief.* Omaha, NE: A Center Corporation Resource.

Mellonic, B., & R. Ingpen. (1983). *Lifetimes--the beautiful way to explain death to children.* Toronto: Bantam Books

Rofes, E. E., ed. (1985). *The kids book about death and dying, by kids for kids.* Boston: Little Brown & Co.

Silverman, J. (1999). *Help me say goodbye--activities for helping kids cope when a special person dies.* Minneapolis, MN: Fairview Press.

Wolfelt, A. D. (2000). *Helping the grieving child's heart--100 practical ideas for families, friends, & caregivers.* Fort Collins, CO: The Center for Loss and Life Transition.